YORKSHIRE

On Holiday

A nostalgic look back at special times through personal memories

RON FREETHY

Dalesman

First published in 2013 by Dalesman
an imprint of
Country Publications Ltd
The Water Mill, Broughton Hall
Skipton, North Yorkshire BD23 3AG
www.dalesman.co.uk

Text © Ron Freethy 2013
Illustrations © copyright holders 2013

ISBN 978-1-85568-318-1

Printed in China by 1010 Printing Printing International Ltd.

Contents

Author's introduction 4

Origins of Yorkshire Holidays 5
Holy days to holidays • pace-egg plays • Christmas • Rushbearing • Plough Monday • Wakes holidays • All the fun of the fair • Travelling menageries • Lee Gap Fair • Menston Feast • Castleford Feast • Hull Fair • The Great Alzana • Tittlecock Fair

Holiday Travel 22
Rail outings • camp coach holidays • the early days of caravanning • caravanning memories • caravan holidays with a difference • heyday of Kearby Sands • messing about on boats • canal trips • steamer outings • charabanc trips

Staithes & Runswick Bay 38
Friendliness of Yorkshire fishing communities • potted history of crab and lobster pots • happy memories of Staithes • fishermen's ganseys • the fishing village that time has forgotten • family holidays in Runswick Bay

Whitby 52
Facts and fictions • crab lunches with granddad • a special place to visit • hunting for pirates' graves • the fishing fleet sets sail • Miss Whitby • the jet set

Scarborough & Robin Hood's Bay 64
Robin Hood's Bay • the Sea Urchin Man • a little history of Scarborough • royal patronage • Scarborough Down Under • Sunday concerts at Peasholm Park • naval battles on Peasholm Park Lake • Italian ice cream parlours • Scarborough by rail • a fishy business • taking in a Pierrot show • a towering achievement • first holiday at Scarborough • 'I likes Scarborough I does'

Fun in Filey 84
The Filey season • elegance personified • the children's town • cobling and doddling • Semadeni & Sons for the best cakes • family fun at Butlin's • 'Aaw, do we have to go home?' • happy memories of Butlin's holidays • Primrose Valley

Bridlington & Flamborough 96
The Great Gale • harbourside and history • horse-drawn carriage trips • home-made ice cream • 'Bridlington, a brilliant butterfly of a town' • tempted by the amusement arcades • Flamborough

Holderness 108
Hornsea • the Seaside School • Skipsea • a build-your-own holiday home • Skipsea rain or shine

The Dales and Moors 115
A right royal holiday in Wharfedale • monastic meanderings • brass banding at Hardraw • memories of Roger's Lido • time for a quick pint • school camp holidays • 'Young, Strong and Free' • holidays with pay

Acknowledgements 128

Introduction

In this, the second volume in Dalesman's 'Yorkshire Nostalgia' series, I trace the history of holidays for Yorkshire working folk. These days we all still look forward to our holidays, even at a time when cars are at our disposal and we have the weekends free.

Just imagine what it was like in the days when Yorkshire folk worked long and hard, often in physically demanding environments. At one time even a single day's rest was a godsend. Over the years, transport by rail and road became easier. Then came one week and two weeks' holiday, and finally holidays with pay.

Everyone who has enjoyed a holiday in Yorkshire over the years has been aware of just how friendly and helpful the local residents can be. Over many years I have been lucky enough to have made contact with lots of local people, especially the fisherfolk. The Normandale family of Scarborough, for example, have for generations been deep-sea fishermen. These people really are the 'salt of the sea', and, as I trawled my own way through the nostalgic memories of Yorkshire folk on holiday, I treasured the vivid reminiscences provided by people like the Normandale family.

This is not an academic book but one recording the memories of Yorkshire folk, often in their own words. So, finally, my thanks must go to the folk of Yorkshire who have over the years saved up their hard-earned 'brass' for their welcome break and 'gorrit spent'.

Ron Freethy

Author's note:

During the preparation of this book I have been given both help and encouragement from many friends and family. I do, however, owe a particular debt of gratitude to the contributors to *Dalesman* and especially *Down Your Way* magazine, who are mentioned in the text by name or acknowledged on page 128.

I am grateful to Keith and Mary Hall for allowing me free use of their vast collection of postcards.

To my wife Marlene, I am always conscious of her help in processing my hard-to-read handwriting, and her advice in grammar and spell checking.

Handing over a manuscript and images is one thing, but editing and designing any book is another skill altogether. I owe thanks to the editor and designer at Dalesman, who have worked up my original material into a book of which I am proud to be associated.

Origins of Yorkshire Holidays

Holy days to holidays

Helter skelter ©Kirklees Image Archive

The concept of whole communities going on holiday at the same time developed as a direct result of the Industrial Revolution. Prior to this, only periods such as Christmas and Easter could be regarded as holidays, but these were more of a respite from the daily grind; they really were 'holy days'.

These periods were excuses for a good old 'knees-up' and the joyful memories of these former times are now regarded as quaint old customs. In their day these periods were much more serious occasions than nowadays.

Above *1950s circus big top*

Pace-egg plays

Formerly, villages (there were very few large towns in those days) provided their own entertainment centred upon the Church. Thankfully a few of these customs have either stood the test of time or have been revived. One of these survivals is the pace-egg play performed in the village of Midgley near Halifax over Easter (usually Good Friday).

The scholars of Midgley School now take an eager and energetic part in the pace-egg performance. Irene

The Midgley Race Eggers

Mallison of Hebden Bridge remembers that in 1938 "The children were trained by my uncle William Henry Harwood who used to visit the school each year a few weeks before Easter to teach them. Uncle Henry was a Midgley man born in 1885 and was mainly responsible for the revival of the play in the 1930s. The event was transferred to Calder High School in Mytholmroyd in 1951."

Keith Newbitt "took part in the first three Midgley performances after it was taken on by Calder High School in 1950. Pace-egg plays are just one of several 'miming' plays which were once widespread throughout the country. It is a hero-combat type of play where there are fights between combatant knights one of whom is either killed or injured. A doctor is then called who soon affects a miracle cure. The present Midgley play is thought to have originated more than 300 years ago and the fact that it is a victory of good over evil probably accounts for its performance on a Good Friday."

Christmas

Fairground swings ©Kirklees Image Archive

Christmas was also a valuable holiday period and was an amalgam of religious ardour and wild celebrations fuelled by the demon drink. A feature of this time was the performances of the 'mummers' which were enjoyed in almost every village. These were rudely interrupted during the Cromwellian period in the 1650s when all form of fun was regarded as a deadly sin. Up until that time the Church and fun had usually mixed very well, and nowhere is this better illustrated than in the rushbearing festivals which have survived — or perhaps better to say 'revived' — in some villages. The ceremony has been part of the Saddleworth area for centuries.

Biddalls travelling show circa 1904 ©David Eve

Rushbearing

In the old days, churches did not have stone floors but were just flattened areas of earth. Each year the floor was covered with rushes and sweet-smelling herbs. All the able-bodied villagers went out into the countryside to gather vegetation and take it to the church. Some of the rushes were carried in a procession of decorated carts, and during the rushbearing 'holiday' the carts competed to decide upon the best float. Even the horses pulling the cart were seen at their best.

The church provided refreshments for the workers and ensured that a good time was enjoyed by all. Morris dancing was a feature, as was boxing and wrestling, and there were lots of market stalls. Apart from spring cleaning the church, there was a real holiday atmosphere around the village.

Rushbearing in the Pennines in the 1890s:
Above *Middleton on the Lancashire side*
Left *Saddleworth on the Yorkshire side*

Top *Rushbearing in the 1870s. This was not just a tradition but was essential to keep the churches clean. The work also involved having fun on what was a true 'Holy Day'*

Plough Monday

Another excuse for a holiday was what was known as Plough Monday. Traditionally this took place on the first Monday after 6th January; this was the first working day after the twelfth day of Christmas. The ceremony involved has long been forgotten but thankfully is still celebrated at Goathland in North Yorkshire.

Just how much actual work was done on this day is debateable because this involved the ritual of dragging around a decorated plough festooned with coloured ribbons which was taken into the church. After being blessed, the plough was paraded through the village.

The plough itself was sometimes called the 'fool' but its more usual name was the 'white plough'; the lads pulling the plough were called 'Jacks'.

Once it had been well and truly blessed, the plough went on a tour through the village and collected money for church funds. Anyone refusing to pay or provide refreshments — usually liquid — was in danger of having their garden ploughed up.

Looking at the churchwarden's accounts it seems that the money collected paid for altar candles to be kept burning all the year round. Once light faded it really was 'holiday time' as fun took over, and drinking, eating, dancing and performing plays took centre stage.

Showmen on the move ©circus-entertainer.co.uk

Wakes holidays

There were also a few excuses for a day off and a party, but these had a sad side to them. These were the 'wakes holidays', when time off was given to remember the death of a prominent citizen. The 'wake' or funeral service was followed by a free meal and a day or perhaps two away from the daily toil. This was probably the origin of Wakes Weeks and in Yorkshire these were called 'feasts'.

A gypsy wagon, or vardo, in the 1960s

All the fun of the fair

There were also the long-awaited holidays in the form of visiting fairs which travelled from one traditional location to another.

W E Oates of Bradford recalls his joy as the fair arrived:

"As a penniless urchin in the 1930s, my life in the hill top village of Queensbury had all the usual great experiences of village life, bursting tar bubbles in the road on a hot summer's day and hearing that the fair was on its way. Waiting and watching for the first steam traction engine coming up the road pulling six trailers all at once and turning into the fair field. Two other traction engines and trailers followed, and we could watch all of the build-up. In the evenings, with the engines running to power the lights and the rides with dazzling colours like we had never seen before, it was magic."

Two young ladies at Castleford Feast
©D Morrison/Castleford Library

Travelling menageries

Mavis Hollingsworth remembers that "Sheffield caught jungle fever in late 1910 when a huge travelling menagerie paid its annual visit. Here were a hundred lions and tigers, encamped in a run-down area of the city for six months. This event was billed as 'the greatest zoological garden in the whole world."

The event attracted one million and a quarter visitors during its residency. It was a cross between a circus and a zoo, and looking at this with 'modern eyes' the animals were not well cared for.

At this time Sheffield was home to a very famous elephant. Lizzie heaved heavy loads of steel around Thomas Ward's steel factory during the First World War. She attracted many visitors.

There was a local saying that anyone who was heavy laden was said to be 'done up like Tommy Ward's elephant'. There was a mischievous streak to Lizzie who once ate a schoolboy's cap, and was adept at pushing her trunk into open kitchen windows and helping herself to food.

Lizzie the elephant

Lee Gap Fair

An oil painting of Lee Gap Fair in olden times

Lee Gap Fair is one of the oldest and most interesting of those fairs which operated in Yorkshire. Howard Wollin of Doncaster remembers it well:

"Lee Gap Fair is thought by many people to have the country's oldest charter, given by King Stephen in 1136. The fair lasted for three days during August and then for three more days in September. In the Middle Ages it was essentially a woollen cloth fair; visitors travelled to the village from all over Britain and Europe. There was also a good deal of buying and selling of horses.

"By the time I was born in 1946 only horses were being traded. However, what captivated me more than the horse fair was the funfair. I crossed the road to watch the showmen putting together their rides, like gigantic puzzles that eventually took shape as Noah's Arks, dodgems, steam yachts, a circus, dozens of side shows and roll-a-penny stalls where you were never satisfied until all your precious bits of copper had disappeared into the stall-holders' pockets.

"At one time the fair was a scene of some violence with lots of drunkenness and fisticuffs, but things have been more peaceful in recent years."

Visitors to Lee Gap Fair in 1908; the fair fields on the right are now completely built over

Menston Feast

Mike Crossley of Bradford has clear memories of Menston Feast:

"I feel very ancient when I say that my annual visit to the fairground was in the late 1920s and early 1930s. This was held in a large field next to the Fox and Hounds pub near to the junction of the Ilkley and Otley roads. Entering this fairground from the main road, you first passed several big traction engines belching smoke and flywheels spinning, before walking into this scene of stalls and sideshows with loud music and coloured lights. At that time the two centrepieces were the large roundabouts and the flying chairs.

"Like too many other things the fair has long gone, but how good it is to remember."

Welsh ponies for sale at Lee Gap Fair in the 1960s

Stained-glass window in St Mary's Church depicting Lee Gap Fair in the Middle Ages, © Peter Aldred

Castleford Feast

Tony Haggard of York has vivid recollections of Castleford Feast:

"It always took place over the Whitsuntide holidays and we always went on Whit Monday. The feast took place on Castle Fields, directly opposite the railway station. What a sight greeted you. First there was the noise; steam organs blared forth, interspersed with the thud of giant steam engines which generated electricity. Then there was a smell of the steam engines, smoke and hot oil; and with all this was the excited chatter of parents, children and courting couples.

"There were swing boats, roll-a-penny stalls, shooting galleries and a flea circus. You could have your fortune told and there were all sorts of attractions set among the roundabouts.

"I went with my father to the Wall of Death and I was amazed at how brave the motorcyclists were. We climbed some stairs until we were looking over the edge of a kind of giant wooden cylinder. The 'death riders' were experts at judging their speeds; too fast or too slow meant that they would fall off and be injured or killed, but thankfully we never saw this happen."

below On the dodgems at Castleford Feast
©D Morrison/Castleford Library

right 'Prize Every Time' stall at Castleford Feast

Hull Fair

Geoffrey Ward has fond memories of 'all the fun at Hull fair':

"When I was much younger in the early 1950s our annual treat was a visit to Hull Fair. We could hear it long before we could see it, but what was excitingly visible was the coloured glow from the fairground lights.

"We always walked along the street by the side of the fairground entrance. The rows of terraced houses had attractions of their own. Every so often, where the front

Hull Fair, on the merry-go-round ©Hull Daily Mail Publications Ltd

doors were set back in short passages, bead curtains were hung up and fortune tellers lurked inside the dimly lit spaces, and the front of the hired houses were festooned with posters pronouncing the great mystic powers of 'Gypsy Rose Lee'.

Then it was into the fair which was a rainbow of misty colours. One thing that always impressed one was the steam yachts. How did people not fall off as they hung on to nets at the end of each of the swinging areas?

"I also remember going into what I would call freak shows; there was a goat with six legs, a two-headed chicken and the world's smallest woman.

"But the thing I remember most about this winter fair was Father Christmas. It was a mite confusing for a young lad to see a Father Christmas around nearly every corner. I soon guessed that they were not all real. I always had a present from one of these whiskered wonders — obviously paid for by my parents — and this made a marvellous end to a day which I still remember with affection."

Hull Fair, the big wheel
©Hull Daily Mail
Publications Ltd

19

The Great Alzana

The greatest tightrope artist of his generation began his working life in the mines at Maltby and Thurcroft, and used to say that walking the high wire was safer than being down the pit.

From the late 1940s to mid-'60s Harold Davis (alias the Great Alzana, an amalgam of his nickname Al, his sister's middle name Annie, with a Z thrown in to make it interesting) was a star fixture of the world's biggest circus, Ringling Brothers, Barnum and Bailey.

Considered a daredevil for working without a balancing pole or safety net, he learned his trade early, on a low wire at his Maltby home. By the age of six Harold was entertaining audiences at local fetes. During World War Two, he still found time at night to practise on a wire in his garden if the moon was bright enough. In 1946, Harold was spotted by a Ringling Brothers' talent scout; within a year he was top billing in their 'Greatest Show on Earth'. During his forty years' career Harold broke arms, legs, wrists and ankles, and even his back. He was inducted into the Circus Hall of Fame in 1991, and died aged eighty-three in 2001.

The Great Alzana - Harold Davis and sister Elsie practise at home in the mid-1940s

Tittlecock Fair

Another nostalgic fair was the one at Conisborough near Doncaster which is fondly remembered by Anne Watson of Leeds:

"The fair arrived over the Easter weekend and we used to go to it as a family treat in the 1950s. It was called Tittlecock Fair and at its height there were two fields chock-full of excitement. There were rides which we could consider to be very tame these days, like dodgems, a waltzer and a carousel, as well as genteel but very magic roundabouts for the younger children.

"There were sideshows with such sights as the world's hairiest woman, the tattooed lady and a calf with two heads; Gypsy Rose Lee had a tent where you could cross her palm with silver and have your fortune told.

"You could try to throw ping-pong balls into goldfish bowls, darts into playing cards which seemed to be miles away, as well as trying to toss small metal rings onto sticks. You could win a prize which was almost always a goldfish in a plastic bag.

"You could eat toffee apples, sausages, roast potatoes, chestnuts and follow this up with candy floss.

"In our mining village it was a holiday at home all in the space of a couple of days."

People loved their fairs and feasts, and it is easy to see how holidays further afield were so much looked forward to. These had to wait for the arrival of first trains and then buses and finally cars before the purpose-built holiday resorts could evolve and provide frolics and fun for those who had saved enough money to get there and stay there. In the summer it seemed that all Yorkshire was on holiday.

Holiday Travel

Outings by rail

The change from occasional seasonal fairs to organised trips to the seaside as a regular event had to wait until the onset of cheap railway travel.

From from the 1860s onwards, the railway companies realised that substantial profits could be generated by running holiday specials, which eventually led to the famous Scarborough Flier. Colourfully inviting posters were features of all railway stations, and eventually improved carriage designs incorporated framed pictures of resorts.

Rail outings were a feature of the holiday period for Yorkshire folk in the 1890s

Charabanc trips were popular as early as 1912. These two 18-seater Thorneycrofts are ready to set off, full of eager passengers.

24

©Greg Norden Collection

Camp coach holidays

Bucket and spade at the ready for Beth Belshaw, at the seaside in the 1950s, with brother Ron and dad

Many if not all, holidaymakers, have either considered or actually enjoyed a caravan holiday. These days, however, this is dependent upon having a car.

I remember in the 1950s when our next-door neighbours Derek and Barbara Tranmer were planning their holidays: Yorkshire was their chosen destination, and they went by rail on a 'camp coach holiday'. They planned these with military precision. Their ritual began on 1st January when they started collecting maps, guidebooks and tins of food. Their holiday week had to be carefully costed and they always ensured that their luggage would be much lighter on the way back.

We do need to be careful not to compare these camp coach holidays with the luxurious conditions we expect these days. In the context of their time, however these coaches were very comfortable, as Mike Silkstone recalls:

"Dating from the 1930s, they offered an alternative to the more well-known caravan holidays or seaside holiday lodging houses. Camp coach holidays gave families the freedom of camping without the worry of living under canvas.

Camping coach facilities consisted of a five-coach compartment converted into a lounge, kitchen and bedrooms. Bed linen and crockery were all provided and we took our own food.

"With Uncle Stanley, who worked on the railway and knew about these things, and Aunt Nora making up the numbers, four adults and two children had our holiday accommodation for £3.

"These were the days when British railways could boast about the spectacular Yorkshire Coast line which ran from Scarborough to Staithes. On that line the journey itself was something of an adventure. The prickle of the plush seats, and the mingling smell of salt water, the smoke and soot from the engines were a joy."

below Ice cream time for the Belshaw children on a 1950s seaside holiday

bottom The Belshaw family on holiday in the 1950s

Bridlington

YORKSHIRE'S GAY SEASIDE PLAYGROUND

Services and fares from stations, offices and agencies

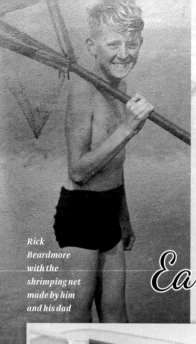

Rick Beardmore with the shrimping net made by him and his dad

Early days of caravanning

Rick Beardmore's mum looking out of the family caravan in the late 1940s

These days we take luxury caravans for granted — indeed I now live in one — and they are more like self-contained bungalows with all 'mod cons'.

Rick Beardmore of Barnsley remembers the early days of caravanning:

"In 1932, before I was born, my father built a four-berth caravan. It had a 'C' iron chassis, with a tongue-and-grooved floor covered with light green lino. The fifteen-inch pressed-steel wheels were taken from a 1930 Bull Nosed Morris. The clock was out of a crashed Bentley, and the roof lights were from an old London bus and powered by a 12-volt battery.

"Besides the cooking area there was a white enamel sink with a length of black hose led into a bucket outside. Mum used to sit me on the grooved wooden draining board and sponge me down.

Happy holidays: Rick Beardmore and sister Ann in 1937

Rick Beardmore and friends enjoying the seaside air in 1947

"Initially we had no toilet and used the campsite loos. Later on we had an Elsan 'bucket and chuck it' within a green canvas tent, but this was a bit smelly. Even more smelly was the weekly visit from Dan the Lav Man; he emptied all the toilets into a big container in the back of his very smelly van."

The McLeod family on the beach at Hornsea

Caravanning memories

Both my wife and I have been caravanners for more than fifty years. Gone are the days when we had to carry heavy water and gas cylinders which always seemed to be running out. Gone are the cold mornings trekking to the toilets, and temperamental showers which either attempted to scald you or freeze you to the marrow. Also fast fading into memory is the boiling of water to wash up, taking ultra-care with gas mantles, fiddling with a temperamental cooker or travelling miles to charge the car battery which powered the tiny black-and-white television; we had to take it turns to hold the portable aerial so that it could pick up the faint signal.

Tootling along the prom

Caravan holidays with a difference

Pat McLeod, now living in Tenerife, recalls a holiday in a 'caravan with a difference' and a real reminder of Cliff Richard's classic film Summer Holiday:

"In the late 1950s holidays, if taken at all, were humble affairs for working-class people. We were fortunate. Dad knew someone who owned a caravan at Hornsea, a quiet seaside spot on the Yorkshire coast. Not a caravan in the modern mobile-home image, but it had certainly been a real mobile home — once. It had been a single-decker bus with its previous life spent roaming round the country lanes of Yorkshire. It even had a wonderful name which was Wits End.

"Although Hornsea is not far from Hull where we lived, I used to get so excited by Wits End that it could have been a thousand miles away. Our preparations would begin weeks in advance. Mother had an old, black soft-topped suitcase with a string handle. Into this, week by week, she put tins of salmon, ham, corned beef, fruit, cream and other such delicacies including jam and jellies. The week before departure was hectic with washing, cleaning and baking scones,

Pat and Geoff McLeod at Hornsea in the 1950s

pies and cakes. We even took our own potatoes. Dad would dig them up from the garden along with onions and carrots before washing and drying them before putting them into a black canvas bag.

"Wits End was homely, comfortable and roomy. There were two double bedrooms, one at each end, and a single bed in the living room which served as a settee during the day. There was also an old fold-up army bed which was comfortable for extra guests. There was a cooker, sink, wooden table, several chairs and a chest of drawers. Lino and rugs covered the floor.

"Cooking and lighting were by Calor gas and I loved the smell when the gas mantles were lit at night."

A holiday paddle for the McLeod children

Judith and Pat McLeod with mum arriving at Hornsea railway station for one of their 1950s family holidays

It's a wash-out at Kearby Sands

The heyday of Kearby Sands

Kearby Sands caravan park

It would be wrong to assume that all holidays involved trips to the seaside, as there have always been plenty of inland sites in Yorkshire where working folk could relax. Susan Horsman of Leeds remembers Kearby Sands:

"I first caught the caravan bug in the 1950s when my father would take us to Kearby Sands, alongside the River Wharfe near Harewood.

"The vans were mainly statics and home-made chalets of rather dubious parentage. All I can remember of this most primitive home is that every winter the river flooded. Dad often had to paddle out in his canoe, and as kids my brother and I longed to get marooned.

"In its heyday Kearby Sands was packed with visitors every weekend during the summer and during the holiday periods. What was there to merit this attraction? There was nothing but the river and a man-made beach built by my father and his friends, who transported the sand from Bridlington.

"The heyday of Kearby Sands was to end very suddenly and tragically. There was a very hot day and the site was packed with people. Twin boys went missing towards early evening and were found drowned in just a few feet of water — a terrible day for everyone. After this, public enthusiasm dwindled."

These huts at Staithes were built as a holiday camp in the 1930s

Messing about on boats

There were those who enjoyed day trips with the attraction of water high on the list of things to do. Joyce Parkin's family were keen rail and steamer enthusiasts in the 1950s. With a broad smile on her ninety-two-year-old face she told me:

"In them days the only 'parkin' problem was us, because we worked in a Bradford mill and went everywhere by train. Windermere was a favourite spot and we all collected photographs of the steamers.

"A boat trip and a steam train journey really is a blast from the past and I love it."

Canal trips

Canal trips were also popular in days gone by. During periods when commercial traffic was not so busy, especially on Sundays, pleasure trips along the Leeds-Liverpool Canal were always popular. Joshua Wren told me:

"Many chapels and youth groups organised pleasure trips, and we often went from Bradford to enjoy a trip on the Kendal canal to a place called Sedgewick. My grandad went on this trip about 1900 and he told me that it was so full that it would not have been allowed these days."

Marlene Jaques went regularly on Sunday school trips on summer Sunday afternoons aboard barges on the Leeds-Liverpool Canal which had been specially scrubbed up for these events. These days there is still a popular 'water bus' on the Leeds-Liverpool which operates between Bingley Five Rise locks and Saltaire.

Round the bay and back for tea; holidaymakers gather on Bridlington's north pier for boat trips

Bridlington from North Pier

Steamer outings along the coast

Eric Delaney's family preferred steamer trips along the Yorkshire coast and "We saved up all the time to afford the rail fare from Leeds to Scarborough and Bridlington. A couple of times we went on the Humber ferry and visited Grimsby without having obtained a passport."

R C Dales spoke to one old gentleman who remembers holidaymakers queuing on Bridlington's north pier in a hope of finding space aboard the ever-busy

Cruising in the old days

YORKSHIREMAN

steamers. He has a treasured photograph taken in 1923 of the paddle steamer Frenchman which was always popular with visitors who imagined New Orleans boats along the Mississippi.

Eric Delaney remembers that "there was a smashing poster of Bridlington published by the London and North Eastern Railway, and was probably the reason that I have always preferred to go to Bridlington for a lung full of fresh air and sail."

Bridlington Quay and Parade

A sea cruise in the old days

Charabanc trips

Until the 1950s, holidays for most people meant travel by rail but there were a few who braved the roads on 'chara outings'.

Herbert Dinsdale was a charabanc driver and remembers those days:

"I was employed by the Pioneer Bus Company of Whitby, and we used to take trips to beauty spots in the Whitby, Scarborough, Redcar, Saltburn and Pickering districts. We enjoyed the open air on a fine summer's day, though we often had to make a dash to put up the hood when it started to rain."

We now call these vehicles 'coaches', and they are much more reliable and more of a luxury than the temperamental and often open-topped charabancs.

Bill Donley of Leeds, who was a railway signalman in the 1950s, told me:

"I spent all of my working life on the railways and travelling by road was a welcome change. Organised coach trips were perfect for my holidays, and from 1955 onwards they became much better organised. We spent cold winter nights poring over brochures and I still have a huge collection of maps."

A Pioneer Bus Company charabanc trip to Sleights in 1924, driven by Herbert Dinsdale

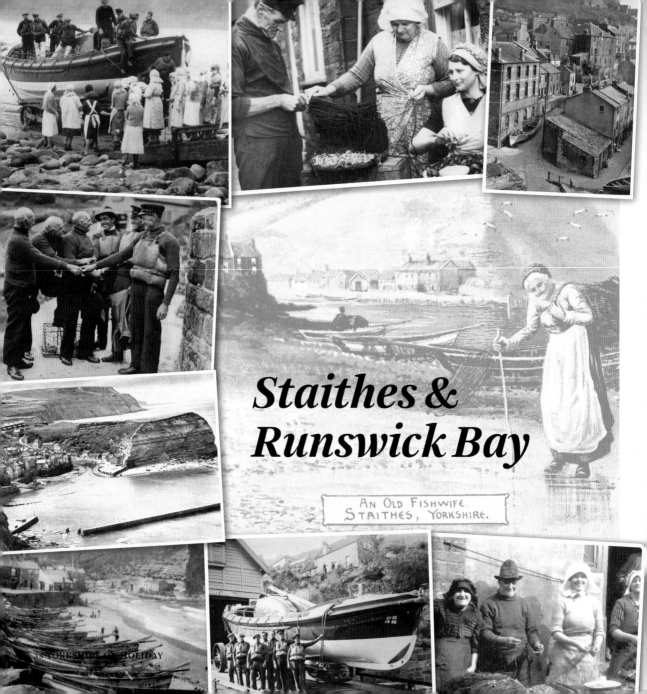

Staithes &
Runswick Bay

AN OLD FISHWIFE.
STAITHES, YORKSHIRE.

Schoolgirls from Towers Boarding School enjoy a sea paddle at Saltburn

I was nine years old when the Second World War ended in 1945, and the first family holiday which I can remember was in 1946 when all five of us went to the outskirts of Whitby. I can still remember the smell of steam from the train and of fish from the harbour at Staithes. Rationing did not seem to matter as you could live off fish and chips, crabs and on a special occasion we ignored the cost and ate lobster.

These holidays became an annual July ritual, especially when we had a car and could explore the area without thinking about special planning of bus timetables. I still love the surrounding villages of Staithes, Runswick Bay, Sandsend and Saltwick Nab.

Friendliness of Yorkshire fishing communities

Staithes

Visitors have told me of how friendly the Yorkshire folk were, especially if they were asked intelligent questions. They welcomed those who bought or ate fish and those who took pleasure trips.

Once you get to know these fisher folk you realise that not only are they tough but they are also craftsmen. Our coastal fishermen are rightly pictured as a race of hardy seamen, some of Viking stock, who brave all weathers to reap the harvest of the seas. But not many of us realise that they are also patient and expert craftsmen, skilled at making and mending the main part of the valuable and often heavy gear.

A Yorkshire fish quay, whether at Whitby, Scarborough, Filey, Bridlington or Staithes, is a busy place where, whatever the season or the weather, there is "allus summat doin'" — men busy mending nets, women collecting bait, and there are crab and lobster pots to be made, stored or mended prior to use.

AN OLD STAITHE

Fishing boats

A street of boats in Staithes

WIFE.
ORKSHIRE.

"JOTTER"

41

A potted history of crab and lobster pots

Crab and lobster pots form the bulkiest items of the inshore fisherman's gear. When the fish quays are buried under these fleets of pots it is difficult to realise that each one has been carefully fashioned by hand, and that it is its shape and size and general seaworthiness which is the symbol of an age-old tradition, handed down from father to son for generations.

In the countryside near the Yorkshire coast we may meet fishermen in their blue 'gansies' (pullovers) cutting 'hezzles' (hazels) for their pots. The base of the pot is sometimes bought readymade, but some fishermen make theirs from five stout boards and four cross-pieces. Holes are made to hold the 'hezzle' bows, the side-sticks are fixed in place and then the 'braiding' or 'netting' is started.

Each group of fishermen think that they have evolved the ideal pot for their type of coast, and the shape varies in different parts of the British Isles. Even on our coast the Scarborough and Filey pots are slightly different from the Whitby and Staithes ones.

A youngster explores the pots around the quayside at Whitby

Staithes bonnets

Skipper Sturr of Whitby, preparing his pots for sea, 1948

Whitby harbour

Happy memories of Staithes

I clearly remember a holiday in 1957 when I hired a car during a spell of leave from my National Service. This was in August and I was inspired to visit Staithes by a *Dalesman article* published in that month.

There was a beck tumbling down the stone steps into a wooded glen, with red roofs glowing warmly in the sunshine. Drawn up stern-first on the beach were the sturdy craft used by the fishermen — the cobles whose design can be traced back to the Viking longboats which once harassed this coastline.

Clinker built and originally powered by sail, the coble has strong planking to withstand the pounding of the sea on this exposed coast, but they get through the water well. Someone described a Yorkshire coble as a boat and a harbour in one. They are almost as safe as lifeboats when sailed by experienced men.

Many of the fisher folk were still traditionally dressed, the women in their treasured bonnets, which have brims stiffened with piping, giving a quilted effect; yet the whole bonnet can be opened flat for the ironing which follows the weekly wash.

The Runswick Bay lifeboat crew

Fishermen's ganseys

Fishermen have blue 'ganseys' (jumpers), and each little fishing town and village along the Yorkshire coast has a distinctive pattern. The patterns have been handed down by-word of mouth to mother and daughter for generations. It is said that, when the body of a drowned fisherman is washed up, his home port is indicated by the pattern of his gansey.

Every gansey is in dark navy blue and the wool is the best of its kind — a 4-ply worsted guaranteed to be impervious to salt water and not to shrink. A quick knitter can complete a jersey in two weeks but most women take a month of evenings or even longer to make a really fine one. In the late 1940s ladies like Mrs Beswick of Runswick Bay knitted the body of her husband's gansey on eight needles. There were no joins, little gussets being knitted under the arms and at the neck and shoulders, and no sewing anywhere. The gansey when complete is the perfect garment.

Most fishermen have several jerseys, a best for church or chapel or special occasions, one for second-best, plus several working ganseys. In the old days no fisherman wore a collar and tie on Sundays, and his best gansey was a very suitable and beautiful garment in which he felt thoroughly at ease. I was told in Runswick that it used to be a grand sight to see fishermen in their ganseys going to church on Sunday evenings long ago.

At Bridlington I talked to fishermen mending their nets, wearing their very oldest clothes. But one man was despatched 'below deck' to bring up neatly folded jerseys. He explained that they always had "a better one with them". All were proud that their wives had made their ganseys and had made them well.

Staithes at low tide

The fishing village that time has forgotten

Nobody has clearer memories of Staithes than Brian Morton living in Teesdale, or Mike Silkstone who has lived in the area.

"The natives pronounce it as Steeas," Brian recalls, "and for six weeks every summer we ourselves were natives.

"It was the sort of place where mum could open the door after breakfast and say 'see you at dinnertime' and not worry. I remember playing around the jumble of stairs and back alleys for hours on end.

"Steeas has not changed much over the years; that pleasantly unpleasant aroma of fish and salt water in various concentrations transports me back to the age of nine.

"There was a natural pool just under the Cod and Lobster pub where we sailed our model boats in relatively warm water until the tide came in. Old Mr Chapman who lived next door to our cottage and gave me a model of a coble which he had made from driftwood."

Mike Silkstone remembers that Staithes "is a fishing village which time has forgotten. Houses which look from a distance like dolly mixtures hurled in a fit of temper hug both the cliff and each other. With the oncoming tide, moored boats creak lethargically whilst at low tide the beck gives up its secrets — trails of seaweeds, shingle and driftwood."

above *Baiting the lines*

Fisher lasses outside the Cod and Lobster

The Runswick Bay lifeboat was named after coxswain Robert Patton, who lost his life bravely rescuing a seaman in 1934

Family holidays in Runswick Bay

This is yet another atmospheric little village to the south of Staithes. Margaret McClafferty (*née* Taylor) Angus has vivid memories of Runswick Bay.

"In order to be called a true 'Nagar' you have to have been born here. I was born in York Cottage on 7th December 1923 to George and Mary Taylor. George was a fisherman and coxswain of Runswick lifeboat, and Mary looked after us children.

"I loved school, and being the daughter of a fisherman my lunchtime sandwiches were almost always crab. Luckily my friends lived on farms and we could vary our diet by bartering. This was a skill which was to prove very useful during the war.

"I had to do my share of what we called 'scaining' which was to prepare 3,500 mussels to provide bait for my father's five fishing lines.

"I was out early every morning to meet my maternal grandmother Margaret Richardson. She lived on a farm, and used to arrive on a milk float with a four-gallon churn of fresh milk straight from the cows. It was my job to deliver the milk to fifteen huts in Runswick set along the bay. Sometimes the owners would ask me to come back later to clean the huts and earn a penny or two.

"At weekends I would walk around the

Margaret Taylor aged eighteen

The women of Runswick Bay help recover the lifeboat

surrounding farms with fish, crabs and even lobsters and barter these for eggs, butter or bacon. I even managed to earn sixpence posing for Roland Hill, a local artist while he painted his 'Runswick girl in a bonnet'."

William Robert McCutcheon of Bradford could not claim to be called a Nagar but he certainly loved the family

Margaret Taylor (right) baiting her father's fishing lines with mussels, in Runswick Bay

The McCutcheon family at Runswick Bay in the early 1960s

holidays in Runswick Bay:

"With my father Dr William Gregory McCutcheon and mother Moira we could come to Runswick from Morley in August to stay at Greystones Hotel. I have a receipt from Greystones issued in 1956 and indicating that my father paid £41 9s 6d for the four of us — full board for two weeks."

In fact we had two holidays each year with the other — at Easter — staying at the Saxonville Hotel in Whitby run by the Newton family.

"We came to Runswick every year until 1968, and I still have fond memories of the village and still visit the place regularly. There is a bench close to the seafront carrying a memorial plaque to my father and sister."

"Since 1951 I have worked as a commercial traveller all over Yorkshire," John Stokesley once told me. "People and pubs were my interest, and one of the best places to study both is at Staithes. I remember in my early days having a lunchtime beer at the little Cod and Lobster pub which at the time was painted a funereal black."

I am not a commercial traveller but I would describe myself as a 'curious traveller'. All along this coast from Staithes to Runswick I am reminded of the attraction of the fishing village communities which continue to attract holidaymakers from Yorkshire and further afield.

William McCutcheon (right) and friend Mark Senior at Runswick Bay in the early 1960s

Local character Old Joe outside the Royal Hotel in Runswick Bay

William McCutcheon on board the Yorkshire Lass at Runswick beach in 1953

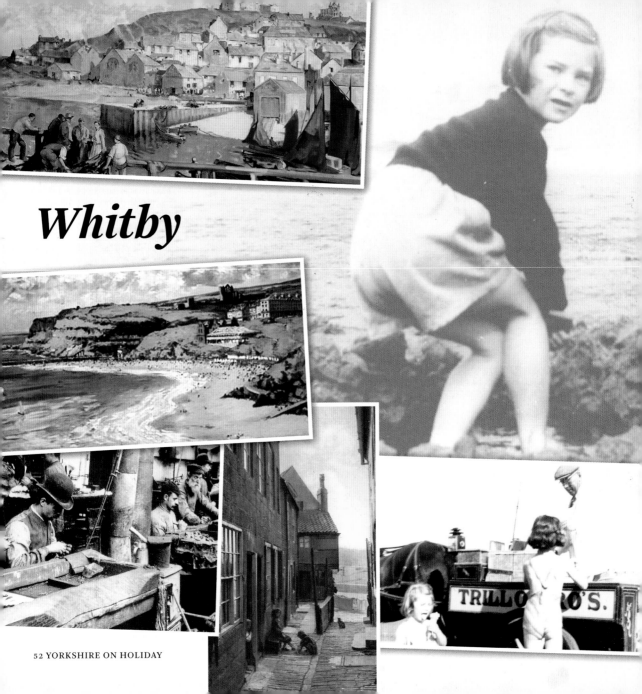

Whitby

Facts and fictions

I have been fascinated by Whitby for more than fifty years. It has a unique mix of history, natural history, folklore and fiction. In the 1990s I was commissioned by the BBC to research and present a series of six one-hour documentaries on coastal Yorkshire. I was given invaluable help by Kevin Barrand, the then tourism officer for the area. He introduced me not only to fishermen and local historians but also to a town guide called Harry Collet. Harry always dressed up as Dracula because Bram (Abraham) Stoker's novel, published in 1897, was set in and around Whitby.

The *Dracula* novel takes pride of place in the literary history of Whitby, but it is a less known fact that the novelist Elizabeth Gaskell planned a holiday in the town to research her novel *Sylvia's Lovers,* set during the Napoleonic Wars which not only deals with whaling fleets but also with press gangs and the life of a Yorkshire farm girl at that time.

Fiction is one thing to be enjoyed but Whitby's fascinating history is another. Helen Wilson recalls:

"For more than forty years I lectured on ecclesiastical history, and all my holidays were spent adding to my collection of photographs and facts. Whitby is not just a beautiful place but is also steeped in history."

"It is a wild and windy morning, as I climb out of the narrow streets of Whitby I see a grey tide breaking into white upon the North Beach, and a couple of fishing boats staggering along far out among the rough water. The wind comes in gusts, with the occasional short sob of rain, while overhead, through gaps in the torn clouds, a shaft of sun light strikes downwards on the waves, and the gulls which sail across it, gleam for a moment with flashing plumage, and are lost again in the grey drifting haze."

Arthur H Norway, Highways and Byways in Yorkshire (1933)

"To understand Whitby's story, you must go back to the moors, turn the modern highways into rough tracks, wipe out the railways from Pickering and along the coast, and find, at the mouth of the Esk, a small village whose chief communication with the rest of the country was by sea."

Ella Pontefract, Yorkshire Tour (1939)

Crab lunches with grandad

Close to Whitby Abbey is the parish church, which is one of the most interesting in Britain. Edith Heald of Ontario, Canada, writes:

"All my family spent their holidays in Whitby. My grandfather was a shipbuilder living in Beverley. I often went to Whitby with my grandfather in the 1950s and 1960s, and we went walking around the town whilst the old man spent his time around the harbour. His favourite day out was to have a fresh crab lunch and then toil up the 199 steps to spend time in the parish church. He was fascinated by the roof, which looks just like an upturned ship."

Wash day at Whitby

Wash day at Whitby

I interviewed Nellie Carbis many times during the 1980s when she was, as she told me, "well into my nineties — schoolmistresses did not marry in those days but I lived for my hobby which was collecting old photographs, especially those relating to old crafts and occupations. I still use the wash tub, posser, scrubbing board and mangle which were passed down from my grandmother. I still follow the family tradition of a week's holiday at Whitby, and collected pictures and postcards of the town.

"One of my favourites shows a wash day at Whitby which was taken in the 1930s. Young folk these days do not seem to like hanging out their washing but prefer to keep their clothes a secret and spend a fortune on electric driers."

A special place to visit

West Cliff from East Cliff

Whitby is one of those wonderful places that once visited becomes a special place, as Jenny Ayley of Gravesend recalls:

"My father Reg Ayley was a Royal Signals despatch rider who was posted to Whitby in the Second World War and soon fell under its spell. My mum, living in Gravesend at the time, decided to sell up and move to Whitby to be with Dad. They lodged with a lady named Dolly, who lived at Raglan Terrace.

"My mum used to carry my brother Brian up the 199 steps leading to the wonderful views, the beautiful church and the haunting abbey. We loved the harbour, and friendly fishermen — one gave us a huge crab for tea, free of charge — and the cosy houses where washday saw the street strung with the week's wash.

"Since that time I have continued to

Jenny Ayley and mum Joan

visit Whitby every year with my brother Duncan. We always light a candle in St Mary's Church which was the favourite place of our late parents."

"They say that once upon a time a pirate crew bore away the bells of Whitby Abbey, but before their vessel had got far from the outthrust ridge of rock known as the 'Black Nab' it flounded with its sacred cargo and sacrilegious crew. In later years by all accounts, the love-sick swain would venture out on to Black Nab on Hallowe'en and then call out his lady's name, would hear this name re-echoed on the breeze to the accompaniment of prophetic chimes from the submerged peal."
Leodian (1938)

Margaret Redfern digging sandcastles

Margaret Redfern in Whitby's East Cliff churchyard

Hunting for pirates' graves

Margaret Redfern of Pembroke has particular memories of Whitby:

"I was seven when I found my gravestone. Eroded by more than a century of lashing North Sea gales it stood high on the crumbling East Cliff amongst the dead of Whitby. The name was ghosted against the blackened sandstone: 'Margaret Frank'. (This was my maiden name.) She died in 1832. There was nothing more. No 'wife of', no 'daughter of'. Nothing to give her history. For a seven year old, finding your own gravestone made a hefty dent on the mind.

"Whitby was to be a future tourist attraction, but for us we tracked down the tombstones of pirates and sailors lost at sea, and tried to read old and faded inscriptions."

"Whitby is unquestionably the most picturesque town on the Yorkshire coast — one of the most picturesque even in England."
    R J S Bertam, The North Riding of Yorkshire (1904)

Dock end, Whitby, 1880

Cornets and those knitted cozzies ... Annette and Margaret Redfern buying ice creams

The fishing fleet sets sail

Dutch fishing boats in Whitby harbour in 1957

Julia Smith of Wilsden also has a fascination for this wonderful old town:

"I had been introduced to the sea in 1938 as a baby, but the war put the coast out of bounds and so it was March 1948 before we had another holiday and this was to Whitby. We stayed on Royal Crescent at a private hotel recently acquired by friends of my parents.

"My abiding memory is the last stage of the journey, travelling over moors which, apart from the road itself, was still out of bounds. This was due to the large number of unexploded bombs and mortar shells which were littered among the heather.

"I wasn't so impressed when we arrived to find the town shrouded in one of its frequent sea frets, accompanied by the sound of the Hawkser Bull — otherwise known as the foghorn.

"When we went to Whitby again a few months later, the sky was clear and the harbour was packed with fishing boats which were following the shoals of herring as they moved down the east coast. The Whitby fishing fleet was moored alongside Scottish, Dutch and Polish boats, and it was possible to cross the harbour by stepping from one boat to the next.

"Each evening as dusk began to fall we joined the great crowd to witness the never-to-be forgotten sight of over one hundred boats sailing slowly down the harbour and out to sea. As the mass of twinkling lights became specks in the distance the crowds dispersed, but we were all there again next morning to watch the unloading and auctioning of the night's catch."

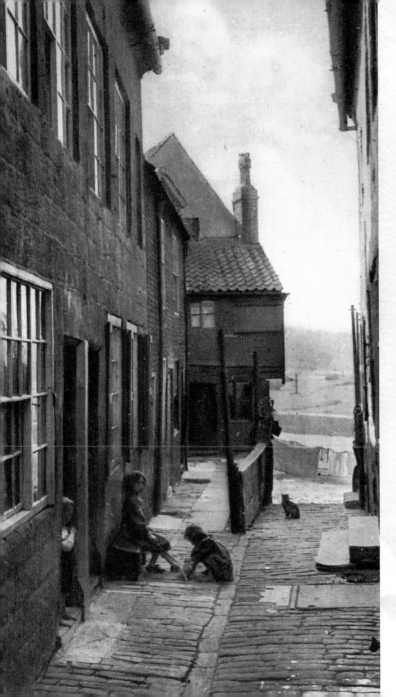

Miss Whitby

It was not just the visitors who savoured the nostalgic atmosphere of Whitby in times past. Susan Barlow, who still lives in Whitby, has fond memories of her childhood:

"In the early 1960s we were fortunate to live in a quiet area of Whitby, Valley Road, when my mum and dad ran a small guesthouse called White Horses.

"With our parents busy most of the time, we were encouraged to play outside. What a wonderful environment to grow up in. I loved stepping outside on a morning to be greeted by the smell of ozone and the sight of sunlight shining on the waves.

"We were the luckiest kids in the world because at the end of the street was the outdoor swimming pool. During school holidays the highlight of the week was the Miss Whitby competition, compered by a master showman by the name of Captain Cooper who was always immaculately dressed and wore a kilt. Captain Cooper had a party trick whereby he would dramatically announce that if Whitby was the next town mentioned he would jump into the pool. The he asked where we were from and we would shout Whitby. He did jump, and his kilt ballooned out and spread out on the top of the water."

The jet set

Brian Noble also spent part of his childhood in Whitby during the 1960s and he told me:

"I always enjoyed beachcombing and my best finds were bits of Whitby jet which I could sell to the local craftsman who made the product world-famous. The trade was on the decline then but there was still some demand. My grandfather worked for an undertaker in Leeds and he told me that the black jet was sold to those in mourning, especially ladies whose husbands had died. Queen Victoria always wore some jet after the death of Prince Albert. My grandfather had a smashing photograph of William Wright's jet workshop taken in about 1890."

At work in the jet factory

Anyone who wants to be part of the modern-day 'jet set' would be better off ignoring Whitby. If, however, you want nostalgia and a place full of history but still catering for tourists, then Whitby is the perfect holiday resort.

Scarborough & Robin Hood's Bay

Robin Hood's Bay

This delightful village, which the locals call 'Bay', has been popular with visitors and holidaymakers for years. Some of my family were Cornish, and in the 1960s when I was first a student and then a

Robin Hood's Bay

lecturer at the marine biological laboratory in Robin Hood's Bay, my grandparents came to visit me and the first thing they said to me was "just like home in Cornwall". After this first visit my grandparents never missed at least one holiday every year to Bay.

The old lifeboat station

Captain Leo Walmsley (centre) with two wounded soldiers in 1917 at Robin Hood's Bay

G.7004.

THE OPENINGS, ROBIN HOODS B

Robin Hood's Bay in the 1960s

The Sea Urchin Man

Everyone was sad when the railway from Robin Hood's Bay to Whitby was closed in 1965, but we can picture what Bay was like when in the heyday of the railways, thanks to this *Dalesman* article of 1959:

"At Robin Hood's Bay railway station I alighted on the short platform bright with flowers and watched the goldfish in the pond. Surely this is a unique attraction for a railway station.

"Then, wandering down the bank, among the jumble of red roofs, I came to the sea and the Sea Urchin Man. His little stall was only a stride from the water's edge, and he scrubbed urchins in a bucket of water as he talked about them. A small crowd collected to listen to his scholarly lecture on Bay and its inhabitants.

"An hour later when I had inspected the new sea wall which was being built just round the corner and enjoyed tea in the little café that overhangs the beck, I passed the Sea Urchin Man again. He was still talking to a group of holidaymakers and still polishing sea urchins. But he now had some assistants. Sunburned children were busy, against the sea wall, washing piles of urchins from piled-up baskets, and their chatter, together with the noise of the sea, made a background to the voice of the Sea Urchin Man."

*Holidaymakers being taken
from Robin Hood's Bay
station to their lodgings*

A little history of Scarborough

Anyone seriously exploring a town should welcome the writings of local historians and none has been a better expert of this for Scarborough than Kathleen Dabb, who writes that:

"Over a hundred years ago, Scarborough, known as the Queen of Watering Places had developed into a well-known seaside resort where royalty came on a regular basis. Many prominent people came to attend the horse racing on Seamer Moor or to take the 'waters' at the Spa. The public gardens were extremely well-maintained, the golf links, bowling greens and the croquet lawns and tennis courts were popular."

*The Sea
Urchin
Man*

SPA PROMENADE. SCARBOROUGH.

SOUTH BAY SCARBOROUGH

A busy beach in the 1950s

Royal patronage

The fact that Scarborough became the major seaside resort in Yorkshire was at least partly due to royal patronage. The Prince of Wales (later Edward VII) visited the Spa complex in South Bay in 1869 and was so impressed that he returned with his wife the Danish Princess Alexandra. At this time the spa waters were very much in demand. Although the spa waters are no longer consumed by thousands, the medicinal miracle has been replaced by a musical tonic inspired in 1912 by Alec Maclean and continued by Max Jaffa who graced the Spa orchestra until his death in the 1980s.

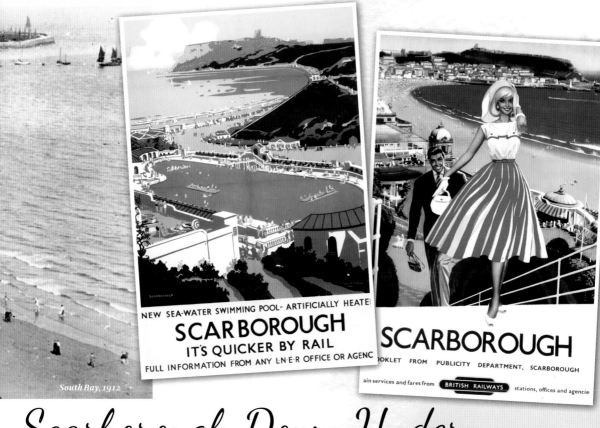

New Sea-Water Swimming Pool- Artificially Heated

SCARBOROUGH
IT'S QUICKER BY RAIL
FULL INFORMATION FROM ANY LN·E·R OFFICE OR AGENC

South Bay, 1912

SCARBOROUGH
OOKLET FROM PUBLICITY DEPARTMENT, SCARBOROUGH

ain services and fares from **BRITISH RAILWAYS** stations, offices and agencie

Scarborough Down Under

As part of my working life as an ecologist I visited Australia for long periods between 1999 to 2010. There I made many good friends and, whilst visiting Greg Lamb, I saw a photograph on his wall showing boats in Scarborough harbour. Greg told me:

"I moved to Brisbane to work for a mining company after toiling away as an engineer in several Barnsley coalmines. I never came back but I remember the holidays we had in Scarborough in the 1950s. Isn't it funny, you only remember the fine days, and I have a picture of the beach which was crowded and overlooked by the castle."

Greg is hoping to return to Yorkshire for a holiday in 2016 to celebrate his eightieth birthday. He is already compiling a list of places to visit. At the top of his list he placed Peasholm Park, and he mentioned that his mother loved listening to the band concerts by the lake.

Sunday concerts at Peasholm Park

THE OPEN-AIR-THEATRE AND PLEASURE PARK, SCARBOROUGH.

The Royal Artillery Band is ferried by rowing boat to the bandstand in Peasholm Park Lake in the 1930s

Elaine Dale of Sowerby Bridge remembers the concerts at Peasholm Park, especially on the floating bandstand one Sunday afternoon "when our son Paul was playing there with the Friendly Band. Everything was going well until the band got to their third piece of music; at this point the conductor turned to the audience and started to apologise, saying that they could not play this as the euphonium player had not turned up and could not do his solo. Just then there was a loud wolf-whistle from the audience and there was the missing euphonium player standing there in full band uniform and with his euphonium tucked under his arm. A rowing boat was quickly commandeered to row him out to join the rest of the band. The audience erupted with laughter when the solo was announced as Stranger on the Shore."

Peasholm Park's open-air theatre in its heyday (© Scarborough Borough Council)

Naval battles on Peasholm Park Lake

Another person who has fond memories of Peasholm Park is Faith Young as the park "was where I cut my teeth in the world of work. I started working at Peasholm Park café in 1987, when the council owned most if not all of the sites in and around the park. It also organised a wide variety of shows, attractions and amenities that were held in the park during the summer season.

"The naval warfare was and still is the key event; it took place on Mondays and Thursdays at 3pm. Re-enacting the 1939 Battle of the River Plate, council employees manoeuvred the scale model ships around Peasholm Lake and the central island with all the noise and smoke of a naval battle, albeit in calm waters. On Tuesdays there were waterski nights. The show included ramps and costumed water skiers entertaining families as the sun went down."

Pageantry in Peasholm Park

Joe Castle regards himself as "really a big kid at heart" and has many happy memories of family visits to Scarborough:

"Peasholm Park was a 'must' and from a lakeside seat watching a naval battle taking place before our very eyes. Guns firing, flashes, torpedo hits, explosions galore. The excitement of youngsters jumping up and down, shouting words of advice. A battle relived, I'll wager, at many a teatime that night."

Italian ice cream parlours

These days a visit to an Italian restaurant is a popular family treat all over Britain but many seaside resorts, including Scarborough, had Italian-owned and operated ice cream parlours and many of the families still run them today. Kathleen Dabb has traced the history of one such family:

"Giuliano Alonzi arrived in England in 1897 and set up business at 49 Eastborough in Scarborough. His wife's family were ice cream vendors and the couple soon had the first

Guiliano Alonzi, who left Italy to seek his fortune in England, and set up the family's ice cream business in Scarborough (photos courtesy Kathleen Dabb)

FRESH FRUIT SALAD

GLORY

SOUP

Our Selection
FOR YOUR
ENJOYMENT.

KNICKERBOCKER GLORY	29
BANANA DELIGHT	26
PINEAPPLE GLORY	2-
STRAWBERRY GLORY	2-
PEACH MELBA	19
PEAR MELBA	19
FRUIT COCKTAIL	2-
CHOCOLATE DELIGHT	16
JELLY DELIGHT	13
ICES Plain or Flavoured	13
CHILDRENS ICES	9

FULL CREAM
Milk Shakes

ICE CREAM

ICED DRINKS

MINERALS

*Annie, Tony and Lucy Alonzi
at the family-owned Harbour
Bar Scarborough*

Scarborough in the 1890s

Happy days on Scarborough beach for the Alonzi family

OSSIE ALONZE.

ice cream factory in Silver Street. His children were involved with the business, and sold ice cream from barrows in the summer and hot chestnuts in the winter.

"At the end of the war the family set up the Harbour Bar. Although the appearance of the Harbour Bar has changed little over the years, the up-to-date equipment used for making ice cream is the best that money can buy. If old Giuliano is looking down today he must be incredibly proud that his grandson makes the best vanilla ice cream in the entire UK."

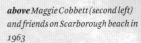

above Maggie Cobbett (second left) and friends on Scarborough beach in 1963

left Scarborough's Corner Café in its heyday (courtesy Kathleen Dabb)

below The site of the Harbour Bar prior to 1945

Just like Italy

Olive Greenslade told me of Seppy Lugani whose introduction to Yorkshire was as a prisoner of war at Eden Camp in 1942. He returned to the area in 1959 and fell in love with Scarborough, even when it was raining. On good days he compared the town with his native Napoli.

Scarborough by rail

Bill Donley remembers that "On a busy day in Scarborough the station staff were on the go all through the shift as trains came in full of day trippers from places like Leeds, Bradford, Hull and other working-class towns. There were also plenty of people taking a holiday and luggage had to be moved from the platforms to the taxi ranks."

Unloading and selling the day's catch at Scarborough harbour

A fishy business

I spoke at length to Albert Wallasey who drove coaches on excursions. He told me:

"I was a coach driver working in Leeds and I always asked to do the Scarborough run, especially if there was the chance of leading a holiday trip and which gave me some free time. I always made a beeline for the harbour and if I was there for a week I would spend time at the fish auction on the last day. I had a picnic box which the fishermen packed with ice which kept things fresh until I got home. Anybody who is on holiday in or around a fishing port should not miss a pre-breakfast trip to watch the fishing boats come in and start unloading."

Taking in a Pierrot show

"All of my family worked at Montagu Burtons in Leeds," Ada Gunson recalls, "and often took day trips to Scarborough.

"My grandparents would sit for hours on the sands to get the best views to see the Pierrot groups perform. The old couple had a tin box in a cupboard next to the gas meter in which they placed small coins which were given to the performing troupes, who were dressed rather like clowns with white flannel trousers and blazers often decorated with large coloured buttons or pom-poms. A white pointed hat completed the uniform, and they would sing, dance and frolic under a tent-like tarpaulin, and behind and above was a backdrop of the castle."

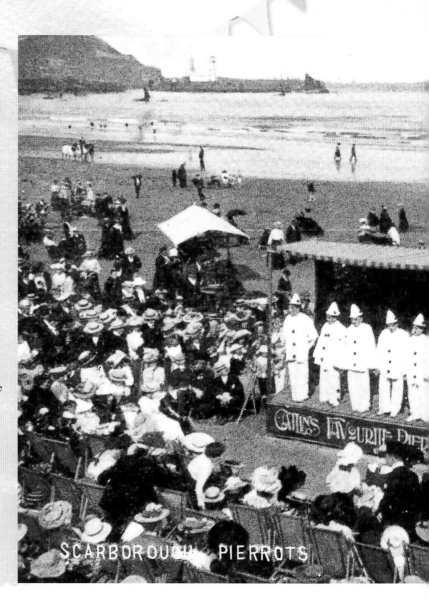

top *George Royle's Fol de Rol concert party in 1911*

above *This Fol de Rol troupe from the 1930s included Arthur Askey (right)*

left *Catlin's Favourite Pierrots on Scarborough beach in 1904*

Warwick's Revolving Tower, Scarborough's answer to Blackpool Tower (courtesy Kathleen Dabb)

A towering achievement

These days everyone talks about the glories of Blackpool Tower but few people know that Scarborough had its tower, which had only a short career. Kathleen Dabb writes:

"The revolving viewing tower was built by Thomas Warwick in 1897, it stood 155 feet high within a few hundred yards of the castle. The view of the landscapes and seascapes must have been breathtaking.

Unfortunately it was thought to be an eyesore by many, and in 1907 Alfred Shuttleworth bought the tower and had it taken down."

I remember my great-grandmother going up the tower in 1902 and she also recalled the opening of Marine Drive. She was working as maid to a family in the Lake District and went with the lady of the house who was there 'to take the waters'.

Creatures of habit

"My Granddad Albert was a creature of habit," Brenda Croser recalls. "The highlight of his year was a week's holiday in Scarborough. He had taken his wife and daughter to the same guesthouse for the ten years preceding the Second World War. The stability and familiarity that Mrs Dunn's guesthouse gave them was important. It was good to meet up each year with returning friends.

"They had the same cooked breakfast every morning and a substantial dinner every evening. There was no need for menus as the regulars knew from memory what would be served on each day of the week and they liked that.

"After breakfast, all residents had to leave the house and were not allowed to return until late afternoon. Keys were never given out. The attractions on the seafront were always crowded on wet days when families took shelter. My mum's memories are only of sunshine."

Mrs V Merry as was, centre, aged five, very sunburnt after wandering off during a family holiday at Cayton Bay, and walking alone to Scarborough and back, in 1931.

First holiday at Scarborough

Patricia Roberts of Brighouse clearly remembers her first holiday in Scarborough:

"It was 1939. We were at war but dad insisted we were to have our holiday. A friend lent us the use of his holiday home which was somewhere on the top of the cliffs near Scarborough.

"Dad, baby brother, small sister and myself were transported in a battered but to us wonderful car. I remember fighting the threatening queasiness until eventually we stopped and I was embarrassingly sick on the grass verge. I was more used to travelling round Bradford and district in a clanking tram.

"We were deposited on what was in those far-off days a quiet country road. The silence was incredible, just the skylarks and an odd complaining cow. I can remember to this day how heavily scented the air was from all the long grasses on either side of us and the sweet smell of the honeysuckle in the hedgerows.

"The farmer's wife was welcoming and supplied us with milk, eggs, bread and homemade strawberry jam. A pungent aroma of paraffin hung in the porch, which we bought to use in the stove, and if I smell paraffin nowadays it brings back memories of this holiday. "We were directed across the fields towards our holiday home, which turned out to be a chalet type of dwelling and it had a covered veranda. It was comfortable, cosy and warm, and we soon settled into a relaxed routine."

'I likes Scarborough I does'

My Uncle Billy only ever went to Scarborough and he always went by 'chara' (until the day he died in 1970 I never heard him use the word 'bus'). On his clean but cluttered mantelpiece there were two faded photographs. One was of a 'chara' trip to Forge Valley run by Milburn's Motor Company in Scarborough. This was taken early in the 1900s at the time of his first holiday.

I asked Uncle Billy why he always went to Scarborough. He looked surprised to be asked the question and just said: "Cos I likes Scarborough I does."

In 1951, when I was fifteen, I was invited by Uncle Billy and his family to a holiday in Scarborough and I was not looking forward to it. Thankfully I was wrong and ever since that time "I have liked Scarborough I have".

Charabanc trip from Scarborough

Fun in Filey

ALEL LINES
TLINS HOLIDAY CAMP FILEY

One of the fastest-growing hobbies at the present time is collecting postcards. I have a postcard dated 22nd August 1924 written by a French schoolgirl to her aunt and uncle in Paris. She was on holiday at Filey, and mentioned the train and bus journey through York to Primrose Valley. She remarked on how green it was and the sunshine was hot.

Family photographs are also a source of nostalgic memories. My wife's uncle and aunt, John and Amy Mahon, loved their holidays and often went to Butlins at Filey. My wife has photographs of the camp at Filey and also one of John and Amy and their son Bob. This photograph (right) of the trio was taken in 1947 and the couple were still regular visitors twenty years later.

"This prewar photo (below) taken on Filey beach is of the pierrots who entertained all age groups," writes Madeline Robinson. "I have often wondered how many survived the war. I seem to remember front left was Tommy, in the middle was Gus, and there was a Jack amongst the others. I thought they were wonderful."

The Mahon family at Butlin's in the 1950s

The Filey season

Filey has had a special appeal as a holiday resort since tourism was grafted on to the traditional occupation of inshore fishing in the 1830s. Family holidays have been the thing, and early on there was a good sprinkling of gentry, including minor royalty, strolling on the sands. The Filey season began on 15th July (Seamer Fair Day) and ended in September.

The Royal Crescent Hotel

The promenade, Filey. The Ackworth Hotel (centre) at one time became a Christian Holiday guest house

Elegance personified

Elaine Granger of Truro has fond memories of Filey, as she told me:

"I have always spent my holidays in Filey since 1959. I started to research my family history and came across a postcard from one of my great-aunts. It showed Bingley Teachers Training College and was postmarked September 1922. Later I discovered that she had studied history and written about the Regency period at a place called Filey. I followed in her footsteps and have been captivated ever since.

"I spent time in and around the Crescent, which is elegance personified. I can imagine the coach and horses of the rich and famous travelling to the resort and looking out for the best places to stay.

"Neither can I resist spending time on the coble landing and seeking out a fish and chip shop. I've even got used to the Yorkshire humour."

The children's town

Doris Cain thinks that "Filey is a children's town in summer. There's six miles of sand for the youngsters — and that's pretty well all. When a family gets here they stay. Visitors don't go out of town much, except to make an odd trip to Scarborough for evening amusements."

Cobling and doddling

HARD'S FILEY

Cobles at Filey Brigg

"I went on coach trips because I wanted a change from railways," Bill Donley told me, "and I also loved fishing and collecting photographs. I remember two holidays in Filey, one going out in a coble and catching mackerel. Apart from 'cobling' I also 'doddled'. To doddle was named for the caves on the Brigg and Carr Naze. The biggest of these caves is called the Emperor's Pool, and I have photographs of these places which were typical of Filey."

Semadeni & Sons for the best cakes

My great-grandmother was an inveterate traveller and made her last trip to Filey at the age of 102 in 1947. She was also what I would describe as a 'fierce Methodist'. Her brothers were all Cornish fishermen and Methodism was part of many fisherfolk's lives. All her many holidays were planned so that she could stay close to a chapel.

The old lass was fond of her food, especially ice cream and cakes. She said the best ice cream was Italian and made in Scarborough, but the best cakes were from Semadini & Sons in Filey. When I was interviewing Michael Fearon, who is a mine of information about the town, he showed me a photograph of Antonio Semadeni who was the first Italian to set up business in Filey way back in 1906.

A. SEMADENI & SONS.

CONFECTIONERS HOVIS PASTRI

Semadeni & Sons were famous for their cakes from 1906

Family fun at Butlin's

My wife Marlene spent her life as a dancer and some of her friends regularly performed at the Butlin's camp in Filey during the 1950s.

Billy Butlin opened his first resort in 1936 at Skegness, and in high summer he offered a week's all-inclusive holiday for £2 12s 6d. Billy was a clever chap, and he always selected his camps close to transport links and big catchment areas. In the case of Filey he knew that he would be providing a holiday for workers in the West Riding.

Billy meets the Queen

Billy Butlin (arm raised) at the opening of the Filey camp station in May 1947

AERIAL VIEW

Fun on the the boating lake at
Butlin's Filey

Making a beeline for Butlin's Filey
reception on arrival at the camp station

F. 42

BUTLIN'S HOLIDAY CAMP · FILEY

CHALET LINES
BUTLINS HOLIDAY CAMP FILEY.

The camps proved to be a godsend during the war and many, including Filey, were taken over by the military. After the war the old parade ground at Filey was flooded to create a boating lake, and in 1953 a miniature railway was built around it. One of the camp bars was said to be one of the longest in the world. There was also a chairlift built in 1961, and at its peak the Filey holiday camp catered for around 4,000 people each week.

Glamorous grannies, knobbly knees, bathing beauty competitions and 'It's a Knock-out' style activities — there was always something to do at Butlin's, rain or shine. Endless entertainments and play, and the new friends to be made, gave the kids freedom — and also liberated their parents.

Holidaymakers always got the best from Butlins: the latest entertainment facilities (even a revolving bar), nightly stage shows, and the legendary child-listening service from nurses on bikes, who, if a child's crying was heard, alerted parents by having their chalet number flashed up on stage.

A Butlin's institution were the always-energetic redcoats and many of these talented extroverts later became household names, including Julie Andrews, Benny Hill, Frankie Howerd (who "died a death" according to Billy Butlin), Des O'Connor, Dave Allen, Jimmy Tarbuck, Roy Hudd and Sir Bruce Forsyth.

Butlin's redcoats in the 1960s

Teenagers enjoying the disco at Butlin's in Filey in 1967

BUTLIN'S FILEY
CHILDREN'S NURSERY PLAYROOM

The chair lift opened in 1960

BUTLIN'S FILEY
THE CHAIR LIFT

'Aaww, do we have to go home?'

Many people have fond memories of their Butlin's holidays, such as Jim Thompson of Mexborough:

"We were a family of five, not large for those days, and I suppose that mum and dad were strapped for cash. Mum was always telling us to eat as much as we could in those massive dining halls as we had no spare money for extras. Dad worked down the local pit and mum knew to the last farthing what he took home.

"Even if I'd wandered off on my own — I could be that sort of child — I always felt safe. There was always some competition to enter or activity to join in. I remember the donkey derbies, the smell of dad's Watney's Red Barrel or Double Diamond beer.

"We never wanted to leave our modern chalet home to return to our back-to-back terrace."

Happy memories of Butlin's holidays

The Gaiety Theatre attracted large audiences and many people came in as paying visitors

Francis Smith of Horsforth as a teenager in the 1960s enjoyed holidays at Butlin's Filey with her family and friends:

"Everything was free and we could go roller skating, swimming or to a café on our own for the first time. Without the all-in-one price I don't think we could have afforded a holiday."

Alan J Kendall of Wetherby has been a lifelong Butlin's fan:

"We loved going to the Gaiety to see a decent show at a decent venue; these were so popular that you had to get there early before the 'house full' signs went up. This was variety at its very best. It is easy to

Donkeys on the look-out for customers outside the Kent dining room

The Butlin Queen of the Lake was never short of passengers

The Viennese Ballroom in full swing during the 1950s

knock Butlins but they knew just how to show you a good time, and they were not patronising about it. They always made you feel one of the gang. We had so much fun and pleasure that on the day we left we booked there and then for the next year."

Audrey Pearson told me that "We went to Butlins at Filey every year for five years during the 1960s from the time I was nine, and while we were there we never left the camp. I did not know at that time that a town of Filey actually existed."

The last word on Butlin's at Filey goes to Jeff Grainger of Sheffield:

"Friday night was always special with families going back to their homes, ordinary lives and work. The 'au revoir' always had everybody in tears."

Butlin's at Filey may be no more, but the site is now a caravan park and so holidays are still a feature of the area.

First holiday at Primrose Valley

"My first holiday at Primrose Valley, Filey, was when I was four." Sheila Cade recalls. "After a bad bout of whooping cough, my mother was advised by our doctor to get me into some fresh air, so we went camping at Primrose Valley, pitching our two tents on the clifftop.

The weather was hot and much time was spent on the beach, accessed by rough steps cut into the cliff side. There were no donkeys there, only on the beach at Filey.

"Parked near to us was a caravan owned by the Milners from Wakefield, who had a little boy called Peter. I still have a photograph of the two of us sitting on the caravan step.

"After the war was over, holidays there resumed in a rented chalet before my parents bought one in 1957, the summer before our first daughter was born. She soon grew to love it, as did the three sisters who followed. The girls still go to Filey when they have a get-together."

Sheila Cade and Peter Milner at Primrose Valley

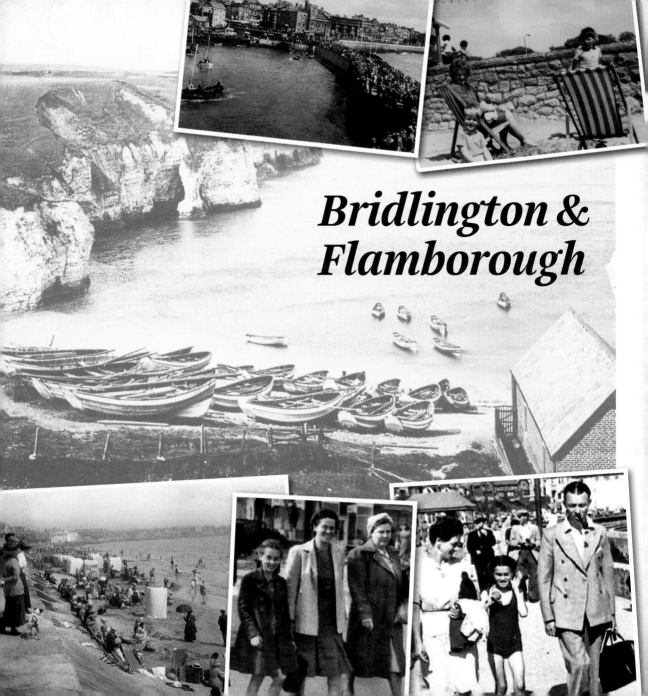

Bridlington & Flamborough

In the 1920s the Fisherman's Sunday parade really brought the town to life. This King Street scene is typical

The Great Gale

This collection of happy memories must include one sad event, which took place on 10th February 1871: a terrible storm which hit Bridlington, sank thirty ships and the town's lifeboat, with seventy sailors were drowned — among them some of my grandfather's friends. He was a sailor who worked on coal ships out of Newcastle and South Shields. He always tried to visit Bridlington on 10th February, the last time being in 1947 when travel restrictions were lifted after the war. I remember that he was late home as the Lake District village where we were living was cut off by snow. The tragedy was remembered by a procession through the town and flowers laid on the graves of those who drowned.

I still keep his (and their) memories alive by regular visits to Bridlington, preferably in February, and enjoy a trip on a pleasure cruiser. At low tide, getting on and off the vessel is a journey in itself, as to call the gangway 'steep' is an understatement. Trips like this, however, are part of the holiday fun.

Round the bay and back for tea ... holidaymakers queue on Bridlington's North Pier for boat trips

Bridlington Harbour in the 1950s

Harbourside and history

"My maternal grandfather often visited Bridlington on holiday from his home in Bradford," Jack Carson recalls. "Boats, especially lifeboats, always interested him and he sometimes spoke with a man called Hopper who was coxswain of the boat. He had a photograph of the George & Jane Walker with its crew, which I think was taken in 1922."

Looking at the photograph of the crew, they certainly looked a tough and capable bunch. In the course of her life the George & Jane Walker boat was launched fifty-eight times and saved fifty lives.

In the 1890s a railway engine was used during the construction of Bridlington's harbour defences

Horse-drawn carriage trips

Maud Jobson remembered her holidays as a child when fifteen of her family went to Bridlington:

"All our family worked on farms, and during the 1950s in the area round Halifax we saw fewer horses and more smelly tractors. I was five in 1954 and we had enough money to go on holiday to Bridlington and stay for a whole week.

"On my first walk around 'Brid' I saw a horse-drawn carriage offering trips along the front. I was allowed one drive a day and as I got to know the driver he told me to arrive at 1.30pm. He allowed me to smell the horse, pat him and put his nosebag on as he had his dinner.

"Until 1965 we went every year and I saved up my pocket money so that I could have two drives each day. I always looked out for the same horse and at the end of the day I was allowed to drive him back to his stable and help with his grooming.

"As I write these notes I can still clearly remember the smell of horses."

Marie Sutcliffe and family on holiday in the 1960s

Nicholas and Pat Sutcliffe on a family caravan holiday at Bridlington in the 1960s

Geoff Sutcliffe and son Nicholas (busy making sandcastles)

John Wardle with his grandparents at Bridlington, Easter 1947

Home-made ice cream

"In the 1960s when our two boys were young," Geoff Sutcliffe writes, "our holidays were spent in a friend's caravan at Bridlington. It took us half a day to reach from Silsden in our Reliant three-wheeler van. Fingers were crossed as it chugged up Garrowby Hill, praying that it would reach the top. Once there, though, we travelled all around from Whitby to Withernsea.

"We had great times on the beaches, weather permitting. I do remember a sea fret in Filey when it was difficult to see anything in front of us. The coffee shops did well out of us that day, and it didn't stop the boys enjoying their ice cream cornets.

"The best home-made ice cream I ever tasted was in Bridlington, and that was always the first place we visited on arrival."

'A brilliant butterfly of a town'

Very few people have more nostalgic memories of Bridlington than John Moorhouse who still lives in the town. When he was seven John recalls that in 1946 his parents moved to Bridlington:

"Easter was soon upon us and the town

On the front at
Bridlington in the 1950s

was transformed. Out of the chrysalis which had been Bridlington throughout the winter emerged a brilliant butterfly of a town rediscovering its purpose of satisfying the appetites of hungry holidaymakers; the repressed desires of people curbed for six long years by the extravagant demands of a nation at war.

"In spite of bomb-damaged buildings

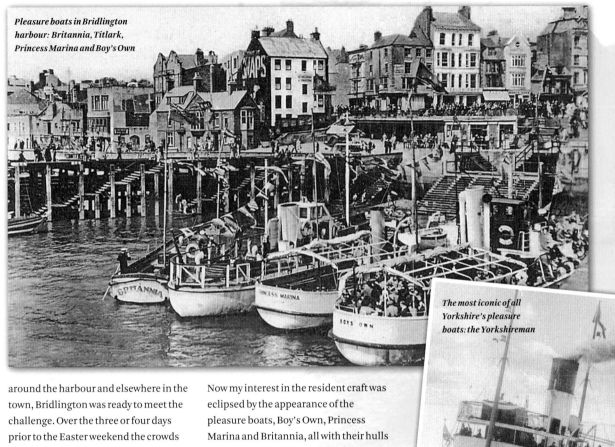

Pleasure boats in Bridlington harbour: Britannia, Titlark, Princess Marina and Boy's Own

The most iconic of all Yorkshire's pleasure boats: the Yorkshireman

around the harbour and elsewhere in the town, Bridlington was ready to meet the challenge. Over the three or four days prior to the Easter weekend the crowds poured in.

"As well as the multitudes, Easter had also brought the pleasure boats to Bridlington. I had visited the harbour many times and had become familiar with the air-sea rescue launches, trawlers and the dredger, Shelagh of Penrhyn.

Now my interest in the resident craft was eclipsed by the appearance of the pleasure boats, Boy's Own, Princess Marina and Britannia, all with their hulls freshly painted white, woodwork re-varnished and each decorated from stem to stern with brightly coloured bunting.

"That same weekend there also arrived in port that most iconic of all Yorkshire's pleasure boats, the ocean-going tug Yorkshireman which had visited

Many people shall have fond memories of the gsteamers which sailed out from Bridlington

Bridlington every summer (excluding the war years) since 1928. This was a proper ship. This was a ship with a funnel which belched real smoke. This was a ship which smelt of steam and coal dust, yet appeared spotless as she prepared to thrill holidaymakers over the summer months. The magnificence of the Yorkshireman's appearance was matched by the delights to be found on board. Accommodation was divided between first and second classes; the well-off having paid a shilling more and enjoyed exclusive use of the boat deck."

above June Wardle with her mum and dad on Bridlington's South Shore promenade in the late 1940s

below Walking down to the harbour- June Wardle (second left) with Nanna, Mum and friend

A Wardle family get-together on Bridlington beach

Tempted by the amusement arcades

Another with fond memories of visits to Bridlington was June Wardle of Grimsby:

"We would walk around the harbour, look at all the little fishing boats and watch the fishermen dangling their fishing rods over the harbour wall. Then there were the pleasure boats — Yorkshireman, Yorkshire Belle and Boy's Own are names which I can remember.

"Sometimes grandpa would treat us to a trip out to Flamborough Head, but although those excursions started out to be such fun, my little face would often turn green before reaching journey's end.

"The amusement arcades would entice

The New Spa was
opened in 1933

The Floral Hall fire in August
1924 prevented crowds laughing at George Robey

us in with our pockets full of pennies and half-pennies. We would do the rounds of pulling levers and flicking the little silver balls to see who could light up the biggest score. And what a thrill when another little ball brought a shower of pennies rattling down into eager hands.

"We also liked to visit the variety shows at the Grand Pavilion and Spa Theatre. There was one company which we never missed seeing. The Rix Company was headed by the then not-so-well-known Brian Rix and a beautiful redhead who was then his fiancée, Elspeth Gray. It was quite

a family affair as Brian's sister was also amongst the cast. Sheila later became famous as Annie Sugden in Emmerdale Farm as it was then called."

Flamborough

When I was studying for a teacher's diploma in London in the late 1950s, I was one of the few 'northern' students. I had several conversations with Billy Dove, who hailed from a strange place called Flamborough. The name sounded so intriguing that I made my first visit in 1961 and have hardly missed a year since.

ORTH LANDING. FLAMBOROUGH HEAD

Holderness

NEW PROMENADE & SEA WALL, HORNSEA.

left Hornsea in Victorian times

below Hornsea promenade in the Edwardian era

When people talk about taking a holiday on the Yorkshire coast they often work their way southwards from Whitby and finish at Bridlington. This is a grave mistake because they miss the attractions of the Holderness coast: Hornsea and Skipsea, Withernsea and Patrington, Kilnsea and Spurn Head.

The Promenade, Hornsea.

Girls from Hornsea Seaside School taking part in nature studies on the beach

above A wash and brush-up for pupils at Hornsea Seaside School

Hornsea Seaside School

John McLeod has such fond memories of Hornsea Seaside School that he wrote a book about this fascinating establishment. Every year 1,500 children travelled from the Wakefield district to Hornsea to stay at the Seaside School. A pioneering experiment when it opened in the 1930s, the school much critical acclaim for its forward-thinking approach to public health, and many thousands of children had cause to love the place. John noted that:

"I spent two weeks there in the 1960s as a thirteen year old. It cost my parents £2 10s to send me the sixty-six miles with the other hundred lads from Snapethorpe High School.

"Across the old East Riding of Yorkshire we sped on the Victoria Motor coach. Only one and a quarter hours later and seen through trees I spotted Hornsea Mere. On arrival at the school I was put into Beverley Dormitory. After a good meal we were led across the old railway line that Dr Beeching had foolishly axed and then onto the beach, where there were two Second World War pillboxes. This was our Benidorm and our Costa.

A boat trip aboard the Victory on Hornsea Mere for pupils of the Seaside School

Well-turned-out boys at Hornsea Seaside School

"My mother spent three weeks there the very first year it opened in 1938. She too remembers her days there, just before the dark clouds of war came and the sound of skylarks gave way to the drone of the Luftwaffe. Forbidden were the next generation of kids to go to Hornsea School for six long years, because this coast was a high-risk area for an invasion. But thanks to our dads and grandads, Hitler's troops never made it and the lovely voices of our children can be heard again in our Hornsea School."

During the Second World War, Hornsea was not a school camp but an army camp bristling with defensive armaments and with pillboxes fully manned and camouflaged. But it did not take long for these splendid school camps to be returned to a more peaceful function, and boys and girls could once again enjoy a boat trip on the Mere with the little vessel appropriately called the Victory.

John McLeod records one girl's fond memories of the Seaside School:

"One of the things that will always stay in my mind was sitting on a seat outside St Nicholas's Church listening to the jukebox playing in a café across the road. It was a typical '50s-style café, although by the time I went it was into the mid-'60s the song then always seemed to be playing was the Honeycombs' Have I the Right.

"These days it seems that we all have a right to a holiday but until the 1970s not everybody was so fortunate and the quality of accommodation was accepted rather than demanded."

There was even a school song, sung at the parents' open day, to the tune of There is a Tavern in the Town:

There is a school near Hornsea Mere, Hornsea Mere.
And there we live three weeks a year, weeks a year.
We play games and paddle when it's fine, when it's fine
And skip beside the foaming brine, foaming brine.
All at Wakefield come and see us
Though you cannot stay long with us
We love to show you round our Seaside School.
Adieu, Adieu.

The DIY bungalow
(built by David van de Gevel's Uncle Cyril
and father Albert) on Skipsea clifftop in the early 1950s, with Albert on the swing

Build-your-own holiday home at Skipsea

When we take a holiday these days we expect the best. We must be provided with every luxury and be spoon-fed for every minute of our expensive outlay. In the 1940s, things were different. David Van de Gevel remembers the time when his uncle built his very own holiday home at Skipsea:

"In common with most ordinary families in the 1950s we had no car and relied on public transport to get us everywhere, with the exception of our annual holiday to Skipsea. We were very fortunate that our Uncle Cyril and Auntie Marjorie owned a small bungalow about fifty yards from the cliff top.

"Being a plumber he had his own van, an Austin A55, I think, and he would transport us from our home at Lightcliffe

above The van der Gevel family on holiday at Skipsea in the 1950s, with the now-long-gone clifftop bungalows in the background; from left, cousin Jean Pickard, future sister-in-law Brenda, Peter, and father Albert.

near Halifax, to Skipsea. We sat on a variety of plumber's bits and bobs — the odd ballcock, a toilet cistern tank, a canvas bag of tools; no concessions to comfort with Uncle Cyril.

"He was something of an eccentric, and this is reflected in the bungalow and garden which he built and designed himself. He built it, with some help from my dad, just after the war."

In those more relaxed days, nobody bothered about overloaded cars or planning permission for buildings.

David remembers the novelty of the garden which "attracted a lot of attention because of the working windmill, pumping water from a small top pond, down tiny cascades to end up in a larger pond containing a few goldfish. In addition there was a wishing well, model houses, a few gnomes and a full-sized flagpole.

"I was born in 1946 and so I knew nothing of the austerity of the war, but I do remember the magic of those holidays when simplicity was the order of the day. I have a list of 'does anyone remember?' items from those days, including Terry's prize bingo tent on the cliff top, the once-a-week cinema at the old wooden building nearby; then there was the Beachbank shop, café and amusement area about half a mile down the road. There were concrete pillboxes left over from the war and areas of open fields now sadly covered by a sprawling mass of caravans.

"Our bungalow disappeared long ago to make way for yet another amusement arcade to provide entertainment for hundreds of caravanners. These modern palaces have taken over from 'interesting' caravans, some of which were converted railway carriages or similar recycled vehicles from an age when it did not have to be brand new or fashionable, but just merely functional.

"Maybe it's a symptom of getting older but I wouldn't exchange my memories for any amount of cash."

Skipsea rain or shine

"In the 1960s when our two boys were young," Geoff Sutcliffe recalls, "one family holiday was spent in a caravan at Skipsea. One day we were all marooned during a cloudburst. It created a large pool of rainwater in the lawn area. Eventually the rain stopped and the Sun appeared. So did the youngsters in their bathing costumes with their buckets. There were screams of laughter as they ran around throwing water at each other, until it slowly drained away. Simple pleasures!"

The Spurn peninsula in the 1890s

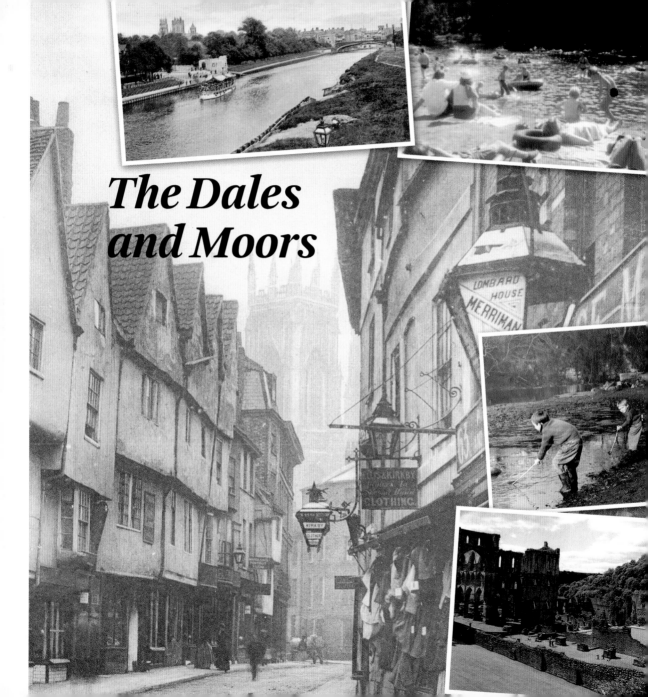

The Dales and Moors

Appletreewick in Edwardian times

A right royal holiday in Wharfedale

Ian Dewhirst of Keighley recalls a really nostalgic look at his family's history:

"On 17th August 1909 my grandmother received a postcard from my grandfather, Amos Dewhirst, a Keighley newsagent and chapel choirmaster on a few days' holiday in the Dales. Although he was on his own, he habitually used the regal plural."

"'Dear wife and children. At Appletreewick, rather showery but very nice for us, storm at Bolton [Abbey] for about an hour but spent our time with Prince of Wales's Motor Driver, he let us take a photo of car.'

"Those few words bring my grandfather back before me with his rather staid manner. He also recorded a fragment of Dales history. That August was significant, when royalty came to Wharfedale for the shooting.

"He sent another postcard home, probably a year or two later. His every statement reveals the yawning distance separating his age from ours.

"'We missed the train alright, we were delayed booking or we should have caught it, there was another at 07:30 but when we got to Skipton it meant waiting till after 09:00 so we walked on to Gargrave and it was very nice so we did not rue much. We then caught train to Bell Busk, after breakfast we had a nice walk to Malham, no rain yet. We had dinner and arranged for bed at Temperance Hotel then we went up the Cove, and rain set in at 2 o'clock about Sunday. They have made us a fire in a nice sitting room, so we are very comfortable; we are hoping it may be fair after tea so that we can go to the Scar and Gennets Cove [now known as Janet's Foss].'

"Of course, as a newsagent, grandfather was used to getting up early, so his holiday, too, warranted a dawn start. Then with more than an hour to wait in Skipton he simply walks on to Gargrave.

"At Malham he puts up at the temperance hotel — where have all the temperance hotels gone? They used to be numerous, but nowadays most of us like a bar where we are staying.

One thing that hasn't changed is the weather, mentioned three times in this one postcard. But then, we have always been obsessed with weather in Yorkshire — we have so much of it."

Monastic meanderings

When I was researching a book and a series of BBC radio programmes about northern abbeys I met a retired schoolmistress called Joyce Berry, and she told me:

"I taught history in several places in Yorkshire, but especially in Sheffield, and from 1923 onwards I spent all my holidays finding out about the monasteries in Yorkshire "In my day, most schoolmistresses did not marry and so I could please myself when, where and for how long I went on holiday. It took me to some really beautiful places. I loved Whitby set there on the cliffs but some of the inland sites are a joy.

"Being a teacher I was never shy of talking to people, and I loved finding out what made folk spend holidays close to these wonderful old buildings which look even more attractive in their ruined but now well-maintained state. Most people said it was the peacefulness of the sites."

Many a happy holiday can be spent exploring the old Yorkshire Abbeys such as Rievaulx Abbey, which is a real joy

Brass banding at Hardraw

Eric Cain remembers travelling from the Lake District in the 1930s to play in a brass band. Concerts were held in an amphitheatre behind the Green Dragon pub with the beautiful waterfall of Hardraw as a backdrop.

"There had been concerts there from about 1885 and everything nearly ground to a halt after the Second World War. It was revived in 1990 but by that time I hadn't enough puff left even to blow out a candle.

"I don't know if it were true or not but somebody told me that Blondin crossed the mouth of the fells on a tightrope. He is said to have cooked an omelette halfway across.

"I loved the sound of the brass bands mingling with the waterfall and the sound of a skylark."

The Eagle's Eye, at Roger's Lido, 1960

Memories of Roger's Lido

This idyllic spot close to Knaresborough was popular during the 1940s, but it all started in the early 1900s, as Nancy Buckle recalls:

"It was developed by a gentleman farmer and miller called Roger Lund. The lido which bears his name was in fact developed by the Harper family who were farmers there following Roger Lund. He was one of Knaresborough's famous eccentrics who went barefoot winter and summer. He was a big amiable man who appeared regularly for the Wednesday market … and taking a 'hot toddy' livened up by the dip of a hot poker at his hostelry of choice during the winter months.

"The Harper brothers, Reg and Ken, began by allowing tent pitching on their farmland just prior to the Second World War, progressing later to providing areas for caravans to park. This quickly gained momentum, and at the advent of war there was a booming increase due to the closure and barbed-wire fortification of our coastal resort beaches. The Lido was to become a haven of peace."

Camping in wartime

"I remember Roger's Lido at Knaresborough," B Middleton writes, "having had holidays there with my mum and dad. One of my cousins camped there during the war, staying in a borrowed tent which was a large ridge tent. My cousin and her husband went for a walk around Knaresborough but on returning to the Lido they could not find the tent. So they went to find the owners of the site, only to be told that they had camouflaged it, as the German bombers may have seen it as they passed over. It took a bit of explaining to the owner of the tent when they handed it back painted green and brown."

Playing at Roger's Lido, Knaresborough, in 1960

Roger's Lido at Knaresborough

Time for a quick pint

"I remember going to my great-aunt's caravan at Knaresborough for a two-week holiday in the mid-1950s," Carole Thurman of Leeds recalls. "Each morning I was sent down to the farmhouse with a jug to get the milk for breakfast.

"During the late 1970s my husband Vic and his friends took his sons and nephews to the Lido to camp in our tent. They both fancied a drink but it was quite a walk down the lane, over the bridge and back up the other side to get to the local pub called the Straw Boater. They had taken a dinghy with them so that the boys could play in the river. They got dressed up ready for a quick pint, and asked the boys to row them across the river but, when they got to the other side, the farmer was waiting for them with his gun. He told them to get back across the river as it was private property. They were ready for that pint after it took them an hour to walk round."

A typical school camp

Inside a school camp dormitory

School camp holidays

Most of the secondary schools in Britain today offer pupils a holiday abroad but not too long ago school camps in Britain were the 'in-thing'. Some primary schools still offer a camp school holiday. In the 1960s as a schoolmaster I took my pupils camping to Robin Hood's Bay.

Ernest Astley of Dunnington has fond memories of his school camp holiday:

"How my brother John and I came to go to school camp in the summer of 1938, when I was ten-and-a-half and John was thirteen is anybody's guess. I think the criteria was, you were either poor or were bordering on becoming a weakling and in need of a fresh-air country holiday. We were probably regarded as poor because my father was only a 'summer man' working for the Keighley Parks Department. We had no money to spare for a holiday but we occasionally went to visit Dad's brother in Leeds.

"The camp was a large wooden building on a sloping site well away from the beach. I don't remember much about the journey from Keighley. We went by train, and that was a new experience for us, as was the lumpy porridge and thick slices of bread with strawberry jam that we had for breakfast every day.

"The loos were in a low wooden building and inside was a row of five or six holes so we were never lonely. Below the holes were tubs which had to be emptied frequently because they were not of the water-flush variety in those days."

I remember teaching in these camp schools and they were just that — a combination of a camping holiday and a school, and lessons were still taught.

'Young, Strong and Free'

It was not just schools which introduced young people to holidays but churches, chapels and youth clubs also provided fun and exercise for the young, as Phyllis R Mortimer of Drighlington recalls:

"'Young, Strong and Free' was the motto of the Methodist Association of Youth Clubs when, as a teenager, I was invited by a friend to a Sunday service at Oxford Place Chapel in Leeds. Its proper name was the Leeds Methodist Mission. This was around 1947.

"On Saturday afternoons Sister Ruth Skinner took the youth club walking in the countryside, and a favourite destination was Ilkley, reached by Ledgard's buses from Cookridge Street. We would climb up to the Cow and Calf, have a picnic tea by the stream in Rocky Valley, fooling round, torment Sister Ruth by stuffing oranges down her ample bosom which she took in good part. We would tumble down into the town for a fish and chip supper (out of newspaper of course) before our journey home.

"Other days we would frequent the villages around Harrogate such as Kettlesing, Hampsthwaite and Burnt Yates, in the days when they were true country places and not part of the commuter belt."

A Leeds Methodist Association outing to Lindley Woods, Washburn Valley - Joe Coates, Sister Ruth Skinner, Joe's son David, Greta Wainwright

Sea legs

Canal trips were also popular in days gone by. During periods when commercial traffic was not so busy, especially on Sundays, pleasure trips along the Leeds-Liverpool Canal were always popular. Joshua Wren told me:

"Many chapels and youth groups organised pleasure trips."

Marlene Jaques went regularly on Sunday school trips on summer Sunday afternoons aboard barges on the Leeds-Liverpool Canal which had been specially scrubbed up for these events. These days there is still a popular 'water bus' on the Leeds-Liverpool which operates between Bingley Five Rise Locks and Saltaire.

A canal boat holiday on the Leeds-Liverpool canal in 1959

Low Petergate, York, in Edwardian times

York, Petergate